CREATED IN FREEDOM

Poverty and Economics

By Phillip D. Fletcher

ARROWMAKER

© Phillip D. Fletcher

No part of this book may be reproduced stored in a retrieval system, or transmitted by any means without the written permission of the author.

First published by IngramSpark

ISBN: 978-1-0878-7906-2

Published in the United States of America

Cover art by Elizabeth Thomas

Phillip D. Fletcher
Conway, Arkansas 72034
www.phillipfletcher.org

Love letters to the beautiful poor and provocations for those who have done too much.

Prologue

We were created in freedom. Human beings across the globe possess a common thread of human dignity and a desire to express this dignity in a multitude of ways absent of obstacles and restrictions. *Created in Freedom* is the first in a series of books exploring in essay form the ideas of human dignity, freedom, and productivity.

In this first publication, *Created in Freedom: Poverty and Economics*, Dr. Phillip D. Fletcher reflects on topics of participation, economics, and the uniqueness of the individual in the context of poverty, providing thoughts on how individuals in this economic situation can flourish as human beings. *Created in Freedom: Poverty and Economics* is intended to introduce ideas of economic freedom to new audiences with the aides of history, rap/hip-hop, and theistic personalism, empowering free thought and influence human flourishing.

Introduction

"So God created man in his own image, in the image of God he created him; male and female he created them"

Genesis 1:27

I love ideas. I appreciate the opportunities to engage with a particular idea from a variety of perspectives and hopefully arrive at a conclusion which most appropriately leads me to love God and pursue ways which affirm the dignity of human beings. There are so many ideas prevalent in our world it would take a lifetime, I imagine, to scratch the surface of these words, concepts, arguments, and the imagined outcomes. These ideas do not come out of thin air. We formulate ideas over a period of time based on reflections of experience. Ludwig von Mises stated, "The philosophy that is the characteristic mark of the West and whose consistent elaboration has in the last centuries trans- formed all social institutions has been called individualism. It maintains that ideas, the good ones as well as the bad, originate in the mind of an individual man."[1] Ideas matter because ideas shape how we view ourselves and one another.

A few years ago a friend exposed me to the works of Walter Williams. The book was titled *Race & Economics* (2011). I love to read and write on aspects of race, especially as it relates to our American experience. I was not familiar with Dr. Williams because he is an economist. Many of the texts I was reading rarely directed me to any type of economic theory. I mean economics is kind of wonky. Needless to say, I picked the book up and read what this economist was presenting. Dr. William's addressed a variety of issues and central to his thesis was the idea government intervention and policies more than racial discrimination were the significant hindrances to the prosperity of Black Americans today. I wrestled with this idea. I wrestled with this idea mainly because I was immersed in reading, writing, and speaking on racial issues as well as issues of poverty with racism and discrimination being the primary causes of the problems. Dr. Williams presented compelling historical context and data to defend his ideas. He was like an angel wrestling with my mind meeting my ideas of discrimination, government relationships, and the economic progress of Black Americans with strong counter moves. By the end of the book, daylight was beginning to rise on me and I left his book with a limp.

This was a good limp because I started on a journey and investigated more of Walter Williams ideas. So like the voracious reader I tend to be, I went to the back of the book, reviewed his sources, and determined to understand more of his formation. What I found was a significant compliment to how I viewed the human being.

We are amazing living beings. We are men, women, and children made in the image and likeness of God. This is the presupposition I bring to these essays. Theistic personalism maintains created persons resemble the Supreme Person God and people possess a uniqueness from all other living beings. Each human being is free from other human beings and individuals discern the distinct relationship with the Supreme Person, God[2]. Many will reject the idea of humanity existing as a purposed creation and reflection of a Supreme Personal God, nonetheless, it is this singular idea which has helped me navigate the deep waters of poverty and race. If one is looking for historical application of this philosophy, he or she can consider the revolutionary work of Reverend Dr. Martin L. King Jr (1928-1968). Reverend. Dr. Martin L. King Jr.'s consistent application of theistic personalism produced significant social, political, and economic changes. We are familiar with the significant outcomes of King's work to include the Civil Rights Act of 1964 and the Voting Rights Act of 1965. More significant than these legislative feats was Dr. King's influence, motivating the nation to consider every human being possessing infinite dignity and should have the opportunity to secure the blessings of liberty in America. Dr. King's application of this philosophy inspired the nation to consider "persons have infinite dignity and precisely because they are created and sustained by God, who is the source of human dignity" [3] This idea of the imago Dei and its accompanying ideas of individuals being free, unique, remarkable, and unrepeatable has been critical to my life and how I interrogate ideas.

I found in my readings what would be called classical liberalism a strong idea each one of us possess the inherit natural right to life and participation as free human beings in this world. Free human beings, those are beautiful words. I found a connection between theistic personalism and the proposal each human being should be free to determine his or her course of life; free of obstacles and oppression. Free human beings who in essence were actualizing who they were substantively. Men and women formed in the image of the Supreme and Free God. It was liberating for my personal life but also how it would impact my professional life among those considered poor.

Individuals in poverty get a bad wrap in my experience because these men and women are viewed with suspicion. They are viewed as being inherently lazy, captured by substance abuse, behaviorally criminal, or a drain on society. Personal experience has shown and history has demonstrated to me over the last decade, those who are considered economically poor when given the opportunity, will move from one economic situation to a better one. Men and women regardless of economic situation, possess a capacity and skill to affect personal situations. Individuals have the capacity to learn new ideas and the skills to negotiate those ideas in relationship to his or her particular situation. Poverty is exacerbated when the choices to increase the capacity for learning, and gaining new skills, are inhibited or removed. Imagine the level of frustration which can set in your own life when you are cut off from new opportunities and growth under a premise others know what is best for you. Imagine the level of frustration which can rise in the depth of your soul because a few prosper at your expense and usually under the guise of compassion.

So what follows are a series of essays. These essays, maybe even love letters, consider the beautiful men and women who are labeled poor in America. These are essays of provocation. Essays meant to stir some type of response by those "in charge" to revisit how their personal visions of the world brought about by coercion are just not appropriate for the masses of people in our world. These are essays meant to expose a new generation of people to ideas of freedom.

There is a discomfort when individuals have the opportunity to determine the course of life for themselves. Freedom demands personal responsibility in the context of fellow human beings. We should pursue activities which improve our personal lives and by consequence, the lives of others. Freedom also demands each one of us respect the human dignity of our neighbors. The Black American experience is marked by a continual clarion call to respect the human dignity of an individual so that he or she may seize for him or herself a life of happiness. This is what my own ancestors have taught me. This is what Dr. Williams reminded me. Poverty is non-discriminatory and yet the best way to confront the difficult experience of poverty is to continue the very call of Black Americans from previous generations. A clarion call of ideas which include freedom, personal responsibility, and human dignity as the triplets of the human experience leading to human flourishing.

Isolation

"He who would dare to undertake the political creation of a
people ought to believe that he can, in a manner of speaking,
transform human nature; transform each individual–who, by
himself, is a solitary and perfect whole–into a mere part of a
greater whole from which the individual will henceforth receive
his life and being."

Rousseau

Communities which have been designated as
impoverished experience a caretaker paternalistic
culture. In other words, they need someone to take care
of their basic needs. The community is viewed as a collection of
broken, disparate, and needy human beings who require the
intervention of a benevolent group to make life right. When a
group of people are viewed and approached as the embodiment
of such descriptors, it is reasonable to assume this same group
will experience activities-absent their input- which are deemed
philanthropic and compassionate.

The opportunities for people to improve their individual
economic situations has been a mixed bag of top down
solutions. Various communities of people, regardless of
ethnicity, have experienced at some point the imposition of
solutions absent their recommendations and by consequence
are directly impacted by the burdens of bureaucratic visions of
philanthropy and economic justice.

Language operates as an effective tool to communicate
self-perception to other persons. Language which can be
delivered in words, sounds, and physical expressions offer
insights concerning the beliefs, emotional well being, and

psychological states of individuals. Our language develops through a series of continuous interactions within ourselves and others. In the context of a group, language works to provide cohesion, transmit values and beliefs, and assists in shaping group identity. Simultaneously, language acts as a means of self-expression. Individuals within a group possess a variety of languages which communicate difference. These differences depend on individual experiences occurring within a family unit, the in-group, and those who do not belong to the group. Individuals are communicating values and beliefs whether we are aware of it or not. It is critical to understand individuals use language to express the joys and pains of experience. Groups of people should take into consideration what is being expressed and measure such language in the context of reality and facts. We should not be under the illusion all language corresponds to reality. Yet we should be discerning and conduct an investigation until a conclusion has been found. Such an approach is sympathetic and reasonable.

In the context of power, an individual's ability to influence his or her circumstance regarding particular economic concerns, people who are in the group which society has characterized as poor, should possess the freedom as individuals to speak on their own behalf. These men and women possess the language and experience to communicate specific concerns and solutions unique to their given situation.

The individuals who exist within this particular economic situation of being poor should have the opportunity to exercise personal agency and communicate his or her problems and assist in the development of a remedy. The diversity of experiences which exist within this particular group-the poor- provides a counter narrative to solutions which are paternalistic, generalized, and have no impact on those who propose such solutions. A counter narrative which affirms the individual freedom of a person because of the unique circumstance functions as a means to illuminate particularities and offers listeners the unique opportunity to learn the complexities of life. The person existing in economic poverty acts as his or her own advocate for a remedy which will align most appropriately to his or her specific situation.

The opportunity to practice personal agency through communication can serve as a dynamic and synergistic event which can influence his life and the lives of those who are genuinely listening. His opportunity to speak on his own behalf asserts his inherent dignity as a human being. Second, he has the opportunity as a free individual to communicate a unique situation shaped by life experiences, environment, relationship, and beliefs. Imagine his practice of personal agency as that of a teacher for those who live outside the economic situation of poverty. These "students" are receiving a unique education on the complex life situations of a particular human being.

Thomas Sowell reflects on the influence of isolation as it relates to a specific ethnic group in a particular area. Dr. Sowell observes geography and more specifically isolation, can influence the direction of a group, even when that group is ethnically the same. If isolation impacts a group, how significant is that impact on an individual?

Individuals who experience isolation because of personal choice or some form of societal exclusion discover moments of loss. This loss can include knowledge, relational maturity, opportunities of reflection with accompanied critiques, or most importantly, love. Love can be appropriately expressed in the context of two mutually agreeing human beings choosing to interact with each other. When two mutually agreeable individuals participate with love as the third participant, the environment is radically different.

Isolation inhibits such an experience. Isolation has a spacial aspect as an individual is positioned away from another individual. The spacial component of isolation communicates "otherness." The isolated individual is viewed as different because he is not viewed as possessing a critical aspect of human personality to participate with the group. At the same time, spatial isolation functions as a nagging companion to the isolated individual. Spatial isolation reminds him about differences, lack, or unworthiness. Societal exclusion especially when enforced by the rule of law, creates a situation which hinders human flourishing and establishes false conceptions of superiority and inferiority.

Isolation while a hindrance to human flourishing still offers the opportunity of response on behalf of the isolated individual. The isolated individual still maintains her freedom of response to the exclusion. While the experiences of outward directed love, communication, and exchange are hindered, she still possesses an opportunity to cultivate herself with the available resources, internal and external to her situation. The loss of potential opportunities due to isolation with another individual or group is identifiable. The loss of participation can slow progress. What spatial isolation can not remove is the freedom of the individual to act. While society may seek to implement policies, laws, and communicate messages reinforcing otherness, the facts remain, excluded individuals maintain the freedom and opportunity to produce. Individuals in economic poverty are more capable than society imagines.

It was previously established one of the outcomes of language is the demonstration of self-expression. A lack of interaction to influence economic change offers little to no opportunity for genuine feedback which can influence the communicator. When an isolated individual is afforded an opportunity to interact with another individual who belongs to a different economic group, the opportunity for mutual communication to include self-expression and feedback can occur. Communication in the context of economics creates opportunities for participants to speak genuinely and learn to respond appropriately. More directly, an individual who is isolated within a lower income community having the opportunity to address a concern or offer a service for an individual with significant economic means can be life changing. Her communication will be distinct and possess characteristics unique to her circumstance, yet this is the situation of each person across the economic spectrum. The opportunity of exposure can result in the participants experiencing a dynamic change. This interaction opens the door to new possibilities which were not available previously, The previously isolated individual gains new awareness about different communication styles, vernacular, and feedback. Simultaneously, the "influential" individual possessing significant economic means becomes aware of her own ability to adapt communication. Essentially, both individuals are gifted with the experience to contextualize communication to meet a particular self-interest achieving a particular economic end.

Second, the previously isolated individual can have the opportunity of improved decision making through critique. Decision making is a process of gathering information, conducting some form of cost benefit analysis, and executing the best course of action to achieve a suitable outcome. Human beings are executing this process on a daily basis whether we are aware of it or not. Interactions with another individual in the context of economic exchange does not prevent the phenomenon of decision making. We can observe in marketplaces such as Facebook, Amazon, or Wish, a decision making process to secure the best good or service for a particular economic cost which will benefit the buyer and seller. In the context of individuals experiencing some level of economic poverty, the opportunity to engage in decision making outside of these Internet marketplaces to improve economic life can increase the capacity of these same individuals to build a decision making process which can enhance individual freedom and greater opportunities.

This brings us back to our initial concern, how will the economic situations of individuals isolated by the designation of poverty change? The economic situations of such individuals can change when systems of isolation are removed and free interactions between persons are occurring to support individual concerns in the context of mutual understanding. Free interactions between formerly isolated individuals can nurture greater human agency, communication, decision making, and productivity.

What can occur when individual men and women are welcomed to participate in the development of opportunities which can impact their lives? How will interactions change when the group is recognized as a diverse gathering of free individuals? What conditions are necessary for individual members who experience poverty to have greater control over the economic direction of their lives? When individuals possess the language to assert individual concerns and move out of the confines of societal isolation, more opportunities appear to affirm individual dignity and produce benefits for our society. Men and women were created in freedom and the free exercise of their potential will be one of the greatest contributions towards human flourishing in the context of economic power and prosperity.

Participation

"Did you hear about the rose that grew from a crack in the concrete?"

Tupac Shakur

Individuals are created in freedom to achieve a variety of purposes. We experience a sense of honor and self-affirmation when we are recognized for our accomplishments and contributions. Compulsion ignores the freedom, human agency, creativity, and decision making of the human being, relegating him or her to the existence of an object accomplishing a task. Compulsion divorces personal satisfaction from the outcome of his or her effort. Free participation affirms the dignity of the contributor and impresses on the contribution a mark of human dignity. A pluralistic and vibrant society depends on the participation of individuals who are manifesting their individual freedom contributing to first to personal satisfaction and secondly to societal progress.

We should entertain this discussion as it prioritizes individuals who are rarely considered in today's economic system. There is an amazing quality of endurance and equally, hope, in the lives of individuals and families existing in the economic state of poverty. Poverty is a multifaceted experience pressing itself on the emotional, psychological, and physical aspects of a human being. There is a daily experience of human beings making decisions which can tip the balance of stability and instability. These are choices which can secure another night of housing or the silencing of a growling stomach. In the shadow of limited choices and opportunity, millions of individuals in America press forward under the looming presence of poverty in the hope of standing in the light of prosperity. So for millions of people, there is an enduring and patient perspective of hope actualized on a daily basis. People directly impacted by economic policies possess significant experiences and insights which can qualitatively provide substantive information to investigations with data points and percentages. An individual's free participation and insights offer a needed check to the paternalistic decision making of a few. Such participation by the economically poor brings about a submission of "good ideas" to a greater glory of free thought and latent capabilities residing in these hopeful and enduring human spirits.

Why are individuals who are supposedly the objects of our compassion and recipients of improved economic opportunities, rarely, if ever, invited to the public discussion? There is the cultural value of success which serves as the invitation to sit at the discussion table.

Our culture has determined a valid and prosperous life depends on economic status, material accumulation, educational attainment, and transactional relationships. Participants in our existing environment must navigate a series of checkpoints along the road of life leading to the economic discussion table. The society employs various communication nodes and networks prioritizing and informing the populous what success represents and the measures of this cultural value. Through successive generations individuals and families engage in this long travel to achieve what society deems as the validation of human existence. The society and culture has made the possession of wealth, material goods, and education as the standard and when each of us arrive at the bar of judgement, we will hear whether we are worthy. If we possess little or nothing of value to use as a commodity within transactional relationships, we are deemed unworthy to participate and prevented from sitting at the table of economic discussion.

The isolation and experiences of depersonalization becomes the particular condition of people who fall into the category of the poor. The poor in reality are a fluid group of individuals and yet policies are enacted to maintain a status quo. A status quo which the designated poor are in constant need of governmental aid while the decision makers benefit from the so-called compassionate policies. This status quo creates within our society tribes of societal prestige and tribes of the economically marginalized. Isolation is intended to maintain power, resources, and knowledge within the "worthy tribes." Those isolated within the worthy tribes use their diverse capabilities in association with the power, resources, and knowledge to improve their own situation while shaping perception on how those isolated outside of the prototypical group view themselves. Isolation can offer the opportunity to develop a whole set of group values distinguishable from another group, namely the "unworthy."

In essence, the dignity residing within the poor, which is the same dignity possessed by the non-poor, presses its way up out of the harden situation like a rose which grew up out of concrete. The circumstances of isolation can act as catalyzers for the expression of new group values and new power using the available resources and knowledge to influence the members of the isolated group. Given time and opportunity, the human being shall assert him or herself in freedom.

History has demonstrated men and women will not continue to remain cut off socially, politically, or economically from the opportunities to maximize human freedom. Our own history has offered a variety of examples of men and women rising up to exert human agency to express freedom and as such, deconstruct the status quo. The slave revolts of Denmark Vesey and Nat Turner announced Black bodies were not commodities to be traded in order to build wealth. The insistence by White American women to secure the freedom to vote marked the end of the status quo of male dominated political influence. The status quo established by government bodies to limit or criminalize free interactions and transactions between White and Black Americans would finally be dismantled by the explosive power of "We shall overcome."

Economic freedom will cost us something. If we want to see more persons in poverty blossom like roses, the institutions, policies, and stereotypes responsible for the obstacles will have to be broken. Our history is replete with examples of men and women from various backgrounds pressing through the concrete of isolation-most of the time laid by the government and our own prejudices- to blossom as roses to beautify our nation. The lessons we can gain from these courageous men and women of previous generations is twofold. One, the human being desires to express the intrinsic freedom to live and participate fully in the society in which they belong. We are not means to an end. Means to be shaped and molded to the desires of a few. We are the end and as such, we should pursue activities maximizing our economic freedom at our own expense and not of others. Second, these courageous men and women expressed in the activity of their behavior the words which represented seeds of freedom in this nation. The activity of their lives in many cases would be at the cost of their "lives, our fortunes, and our sacred honor."

We are human beings created in freedom to participate with one another for a variety of purposes. Human beings meant to blossom like beautiful roses.

Invitation

"Instead of trying to prove your opponent wrong, try to see in what sense he might be right."

Robert Nozick

The discussion concerning poverty in America is consequential to millions of lives. The phenomenon does not isolate itself to a particular ethnic group, region of our country, or educational level. Poverty is an economic experience which can be the reality of any individual. Depending on one's audience, the conversation can move between the statistical economic situation of a particular group of persons to the emotional, psychological, and physical experience of poverty in the lives of Americans.

In my experience the majority of individuals do not want to remain in poverty. In fact, all of us are born poor. We come into this world lacking the human capital of skills, decision making, and economic knowledge to immediately impact our situation. A move out of poverty is initially dependent on parental involvement, some form of education, the goodwill of others, and the intense personal desire to improve one's situation over time. Poverty does not have to be a permanent reality for individuals.

We should acknowledge there is also a countercultural commitment, especially among various religious adherents, to adopt a state of poverty, preferring an emphasis on transcendent riches instead of material accumulation. It is a preference to identify with those individuals who are experiencing poverty. These wonderful individuals deserve our admiration as they exist as bright lights shining on humanity to view the possession of material goods in a proper perspective. These are individuals we should aspire to emulate in terms of possessing a transcendent vision and sympathetic practices of love for others.

We are human beings who have a common journey to arrive at a destination called happiness. The majority of human beings desire to improve their economic situations by acquiring and distributing materials of value to ultimately experience happiness. We earnestly hope these journeys toward unique and specific realities of happiness are without obstacles, inclines, and deep valleys. We should hope as well the gains of happiness by one individual will not come at the expense of other travelers on the same road.

We are now traveling the road of the 21st century debating the appropriate economic system which will create an environment for the greatest level of prosperity for participants in that system. We should critically investigate whether the current economic system in America still has the potency to lift as many individuals as possible. Is it possible another system such as democratic socialism or some form of socialism, has the potency to effectively cultivate an environment producing prosperity and as a consequence improve the economic situations of the individuals designated as poor? Maybe none of the above systems theorized in previous centuries can effectively respond to this new age of technology which includes the Internet, self-service opportunities, and the growing development of artificial intelligence. At the same time, thousands of human interactions involving the exchange of items of value to achieve individual satisfaction has not changed. These are phenomenon which are prevalent in societies and cultures of history.

I've heard it asked, "How did people move out of poverty?" Our ancestors were brought out of the earth, given the breath of life, standing homeless and naked. In freedom, our ancestors created ways of life with the resources available, participated in human interactions to conduct exchanges of value which produced income, amassed wealth, and ultimately happiness.

Questioning the validity, effectiveness, and outcomes of economic systems needs to be the work of as many citizens as possible. There should be a variety of individuals with various skill sets, education, and backgrounds who will participate on a continual basis regarding this work as well as everyday people who have knowledge to contribute. Who are these individuals who should be at the table for discussion?

First, the individuals directly impacted within the particular system should have a seat at the table. The statements and expressions which will be communicated by these impacted individuals can provide the immediate information necessary for the development of appropriate solutions. These individuals have significant contributions regarding personal experience but they also possess significant input in terms of propositions and recommendations. Their language may not be academic and they may not use the vernacular of skilled economists. What they do contribute is the first hand knowledge of personal experience.

Second, an invitation should be offered to opponents and proponents of the specific economic system under consideration. Admittedly, proponents of the existing system possess a special interest in the maintenance and perpetuation of the system. It is reasonable to believe proponents of a system will be passionate, assertive, and persuasive, outlining the logic and benefits of the system. Equally, in a pluralist society such as our own, we should want opponents to express counter arguments with accompanying facts. Thus, in our economic system, individuals in various economic situations, modern economists, and voices of the past should participate. There are voices from the past which need to be heard such as Locke, Bastiat, Marx, and Rousseau. The modern voices of Sowell, Williams, Rawls, Nozick, and Friedman must be allowed to speak equally.

The table is still large enough to invite other voices. Thus, it is important to evaluate the moral and ethical character of the economic system. Jesus must have a voice as his ethic and mandate "to love your neighbor," should have an influence. Also other religious and nonreligious voices which prioritize moral universal truths which affirm the dignity of human beings must speak with clarity, offer objections, uplift benefits, and offer recommendations to solidify the moral foundation of the system.

Why should we entertain a pluralistic discussion regarding the economic system as it relates to human beings who live in poverty? An environment which presents a pluralist society actualizes the reality of a diverse membership of individuals who are united by a common thread. A pluralist society acknowledges the viability of a cohesive and diverse group which requires the participation of its individual members. The best society creates an environment in which individual member participation without compulsion, demonstrates an environment which is fundamentally committed to honor and respect the freedom of its members.

Our American society is indeed expansive enough to acknowledge and ask for the participation of its citizens. Since her very difficult inception, marked with a mixed bag of just and unjust behaviors, this country has within its foundations the materials to make real the promise of a union marked by liberty and prosperity. These materials necessitate the involvement of "We the people." People who exist in a variety of economic situations desiring the opportunity to make for themselves a life free of obstacles, inclines, and depressions. There are people within this great nation who simply want to be free to determine for themselves the course of their lives and achieve a level of happiness absent limitations.

So we should go out into the trailer parks, the towering projects in the inner cities, and the rural areas and say, "Come to the table!" We should invite the men and women who understand living on limited means and who have entrepreneurial aspirations, "Come to the table!" There is enough room for as many individuals as possible to come and share insights which can contribute to individual and societal prosperity.

There is enough room at the table for all who are willing to participate and support the freedom of individuals to achieve personal goals and happiness.

Economic Environments

"I pay taxes, so much taxes, don't make sense. Where do my
dollars go, you see lately I ain't been convinced."

J.Cole

An environment which supports the existence of free
markets is an environment which we should applaud. A
free market environment which will have various
expressions has contributed to greater mobility of persons
along a journey towards happiness. There is an
acknowledgement the opportunity for two persons to interact
with each other with the purpose of exchanging items of value
resulting in the movement of resources and employment, has
contributed to countless cross cultural interactions. Free
markets have contributed to technological innovations such as
the mobile phone and wireless hot spots, interactive devices
such as Siri and Alexa, and customer service innovation in the
form of self-checkout. Where the system has contributed to
multiple societal advancements, it is not without negative and
unintended consequences.

It is important to establish from the onset, capitalism,
socialism, and communism can succumb to the detrimental
errors of objectification. Objectification in the sense, persons
who are participating in the specific economy either through
creation or purchase of goods and services become
transactional objects themselves. Human beings who are
subjects, active participants with psychological emotional,
spiritual, and physical agency face the real possibility of
depersonalization for the sustainability of the particular
economic system. Communism and socialism succumb more

quickly to the objectification of human beings by eliminating the importance of private property, deeming it as a societal resource, and repositioning citizens as servants of the state. At the same time, capitalism can succumb to a hubris which objectifies human beings as well. Human beings tend to organize. Humans by necessity organize around common goals, purposes, and resources to achieve individual and group desires. When organization and participation are freely agreed upon, the individual members and the group benefit over time.

Corporations are one such example of people organizing into a legal entity to offer some form of service to meet an identified need. This corporation will require the labor, ingenuity, and time of people resulting in a service which will benefit others. Additionally, the people required to conduct labor freely engage in a transactional relationship with the corporation. The freely participating person is supposed to benefit by applying his or her intellect, skill, and creativity towards the production of the service. At the same time, the corporation agrees through a contract to compensate freely participating individuals for services rendered. A free market environment supports the human dignity of individuals and supports the freedom of individuals to interact and exchange with each other to satisfy individual self-interest cultivates an environment of prosperity over time.

The subtle lure of success and increased profit margins can create a hubris resulting in objectification. Sometimes through intentionality, but more so by implicit execution of policies, procedures, and influence, businesses can create an organizational culture and climate which can marginalize workers and create situations of steady decline towards objectification. America is not immune to massive consolidations of wealth through income for certain groups of people. We must acknowledge some corporations make significant economic gains at the expense of others through powerful lobbies, infusion of income through tax policy, corporate welfare initiatives, and most importantly workers within corporations. History has demonstrated it only requires the appropriate level of communication, discontent, and protest to bring awareness to such realities. The free market without the minimum societal guidelines can ultimately become a system which turns on its society consuming the people it vitally depends on for its own viability. In the end, we must evaluate ourselves and determine which environment creates the greatest opportunity for human freedom while minimizing the possible consequences of objectifying people.

Historically, the economic system of communism has demonstrated the tendency towards the diminishment of private property and the death of human beings. Socialism, which has manifested in a variety of forms historically and currently has contributed to the maladies of human flourishing, attempting to secure the elusive dream of equality through collective or government ownership of the production of goods and services. Our current climate has produced a growing intensity and advocacy for a wider expression of democratic socialism because many have felt left behind by the current economic system. We are facing the possibility of seeing the state not only maintain a monopoly on education, but healthcare, labor, and income distribution. If the free market does not advance a moral and ethical case for its existence, another system will be desired.

In the scope of human history, economic systems have moved from the consolidation of resources in the hands of a few such as monarchies and feudal lords into the hands of multiple people with no regard of distinctions. Take into consideration the Hebraic literature of the Old Testament and what we read is amazing. The first persons who began with nothing save some animal skin, produce offspring which built cities, pyramids, and temple structures. A literature which begins with persons having no material goods offers evidence of civilizations accessing the surrounding resources to support families and societies. There was something occurring within these Ancient Near Eastern groups which eventually spread east and west producing people accumulating some level of economic prosperity. History can not allow us to ignore military conquest, plagues, and alliances which shifted economic prowess and access to resources. We can not ignore the differential in access, development, and distribution of philosophical, scientific, and religious knowledge which influence societies and how they respond to the existing environment. History offers us instruction, presenting a curriculum with informs our present day about human behavior in relationship to economics. Human beings influenced by a number of factors respond differently and thus contribute to a variety of economic outcomes.

What history offers are persons who have growing opportunities within the societies of the world to access resources and participate in some form of economic situation creating more cross cultural interactions leading to greater access of knowledge and personal improvement. The Roman Empire connected the known world of the Mediterranean, the Ancient Near East, and what is modern Britain. In this growing infrastructure project, diverse ethnic groups could move to areas once obstructed by terrain. In these new accessible areas, new resources became accessible, offering new opportunities for merchant travelers and new customers. New resources and opportunities not only benefited a particular tribe or regional group. These opportunities also increased benefits for females. Admittedly the early world history demonstrates male dominance yet there is evidence of women who possessed the economic prosperity to extend influence and create opportunities for others. The New Testament Christian Scriptures record the story of Lydia who was instrumental in the missionary support of the Apostle Paul in Philippi. Important to this discussion was she functioned as an entrepreneur, selling "purple goods" (Acts 16) maintaining both a profession and household, inferring the possession of a level of wealth.

As more persons experience opportunities to freely engage within an economic system with very little obstruction, such persons have the opportunity to flourish. Where we are currently existing in our societal life is the growth of more economic restrictions. The lessons of history inform our society on the reality of trade-offs between persons who desire to exercise creativity in combination with skill to meet a particular societal need and those who desire to implement restrictions with the goal of influencing outcomes within the same society. Our concerns should consider the free state of persons and how such freedoms can be actualized within an economic system which supports an environment of maximum creativity, productivity, and exchange. In addition, we must consider the outcomes of such environments necessitates difference.

Again, an economic system which seeks to mitigate and lessen differences in outcomes requires a trade-off in the arena of freedom. Herein lies a tug-of-war within the human experience. How much can a society tolerate regarding differences between individuals are products of human freedom, desire, skill, and other factors outside of human control?

Free Individuals Pursuing Enjoyment

"Where relationships are based on consent and mutual agreement there can be no plunder, only reinforcing prosperity, as each works to trade with his neighbors and acquire all the things that make life better for each and all."

Richard Ebeling

An economic environment is the combination of various factors resulting from the interactions of individual members within that environment. At a basic level, persons are higher level "selfs"," beings who influence the economic environment with freedom and reason. At the same time, individuals employ freedom and reason in response to the environment. Individuals respond to the factors produced within the economic environment, making decisions which ultimately extend the well-being of the individual. An individual response to the environment implies there is a level of self-reflection which is occurring, reflecting on past experiences and future possibilities to influence his or her particular situation.

The activity of self-reflection is the individual's participation in transcendence, rising above time within in the environment. Second, the individual distinguishes himself or herself from environment. A tree has no awareness it is distinct from the environment in which it is rooted. The phenomenon of self-awareness leading to a reasoned response for the outcome of an improved well-being is dependent on particular environmental factors. Human beings possess the capacity to distinguish themselves from the environment and through reason and freedom pursue activities which can improve personal well-being. There is a freedom which the tree or other non-personable beings do not experience. [I anticipate an objection regarding animals. In response, the context of our discussion is limited to human participation in an economic system which animals possess no awareness or will to participate.]

Therefore, individual human beings existing in an economic system possess the freedom of distinction from the environment as well as the freedom of response. The combinations of distinction and free response carry significant influence on an individual within a particular economic environment. While particular factors can influence individuals, those same participants possess a basic level of freedom and reason which will ultimately produce a variety of outcomes.

Individuals are inherently free beings who possess the will and intellect to engage in relationships with similar persons. We should pursue an economic environment which reflects what is internally known to individuals. We recognize individuals engage in relationships based on common understandings such as beliefs, values, physical attributes, or goals, with isolation or segregation being a possibility. In the process of interactions, individuals arrive at a number of agreements and practices which strengthen these interactions. As these individuals collaborate, personal necessity stimulates the creativity and ingenuity serving the interest of individuals. A hole must be filled and the soul will be anxious until it finds rest by achieving his or her particular interest. Human beings possess needs and we should have life experiences maximizing opportunities to freely interact with others achieve our individual interests.

Human flourishing is not about the accumulation of material goods primarily, but the acquisition of personal happiness through free expression and interactions with others. In an organized society, individuals should work towards the actualization and protection of individual freedom. Freedom in which individuals can interact to have needs satisfied. Freedom which is protected by laws designed to pursue happiness and restrain all forms of injustice.

We are consumers and producers in our society. As consumers we have the opportunity of self-production or we find someone with whom we can mutually agree to exchange something of value for what we desire to consume. We are producers as well. I desire to produce a product which is not readily available. Consider the excitement today regarding entrepreneurship. Men and women sitting in coffee shops, on front porches, and in start-up classes, formulating ideas and plans to create some item or service of value to achieve personal satisfaction and by consequence impact society. These men and women represent producers and in participation with consumers, each participant will achieve some level of satisfaction.

As consumers and producers, what we demonstrate is the powerful and magnificent activity called work. Individual men and women who have been created in freedom, possess a unique personality, and diverse capabilities should have the opportunity to act without hindrance to improve his or her individual situation and the society.

Individuals collaborating and cooperating to address particular needs and goals are executing solutions and these solutions contain trade-offs. Trade-offs are events which one person freely chooses on her own to relinquish something of value to satisfy a particular need. Simultaneously, the other individual freely chooses on his own to relinquish something of value to satisfy a need. It is very important to realize trade-offs are occurring daily. Collaborating individuals freely choosing for themselves and relinquishing resources of value to achieve goals and/or meet needs. The resources of value can include time, labor, currency, fuel, knowledge, or any other resource the individual deems valuable. There are other aspects of trade-offs to be considered in the context of collaborating individuals, namely location, outcomes, and enjoyment.

A pluralistic society such as America should consider the location of individuals and access to resources. The diversity of locations within the continental United States is a wonder to consider. Moving from east to west, a traveler can experience a variety of geographies, topographies, and water ways. The diversity of features necessitates different decisions, plans, and the execution of activities by individuals and geographic locations. It is safe to assume two individuals of the same ethnic situation living in different geographic locations will cultivate different activities. Our imagination is helpful in the consideration of trade-offs between these two similar and yet dissimilar individuals. By virtue of participating in distinct locations with access to a variety of resources, these two individuals interact with each other with surplus and deficits. Humanizing interactions between individuals include each individual freely choosing to relinquish what is of value-surplus or deficit-to achieve personal satisfaction. Humanizing interactions are mentioned because these activities uphold the dignity of individuals through practices of free interactions. What are to be avoided are interactions which intend to manipulate or practice coercion which deny the equal standing of participating individuals.

The second consideration regarding trade offs involves the reality of diverse outcomes. The context of freely participating individuals from different locations with different resources can not ignore the existence of different outcomes. Individual outcomes are dependent on the existence of diverse individuals and their particular needs. Trade-offs are a necessary reality between individuals existing in a particular geographic and economic space. What trade-offs can not guarantee are outcomes in which all individuals experience equity concerning his or her economic position. While we should accept we are intrinsically equal on the basis of personhood, our pursuits and the associated outcomes will not be equal in quantity or value. As a matter of judicial justice, human beings are equal before the high bar of a courtroom. As a matter of social justice, human beings should possess the opportunity of free association, communication, and movement to accomplish individual goals. As a matter of economic justice, participants should have the free opportunity to interact and exchange goods and services which will lead to different economic outcomes. The final economic outcome is subjective in terms of purpose and value because of the diversity of individual needs and goals.

A final consideration regarding trade-offs is the reality people are pursuing enjoyment. If satisfaction is the realization a particular need is being achieved, enjoyment is the experience of deriving pleasure from the trade off. People, regardless of economic position are desiring enjoyment. In the case of poverty, the lack of a material, psychological, or emotional good, inhibits the realization of enjoyment. While an Epicurean perspective to life considers the pursuit of enjoyment as the absence of suffering, a trade-off infers loss or suffering as a necessary component in the acquisition of the experience.

We should acknowledge people daily are experiencing loss to secure satisfaction and the associated experience of enjoyment.

There are a variety of outcomes possible when two individuals interact, barter, and exchange with one another for the ultimate purpose of enjoyment. These outcomes can include accumulation of goods, transportation, settlement in a particular area, acquisition of goods for subsequent exchange, or destruction of goods. These outcomes when observed have become much of the problems for well meaning persons seeking to address economic inequality. The various outcomes mentioned above are related to individuals who have chosen to pursue these ends, yet are not acceptable to other well meaning persons. In response to these varied outcomes the proposed solutions by elected leaders and political candidates recently has been redistribution of income through increased taxation on the goods and services of participants or the taxation of an individuals accumulated wealth. The opportunities individuals take to achieve particular outcomes are characterized as greedy and corrupt, seeking to oppress particular people. The reality of the human experience within various economic systems throughout the world demonstrates the existence of diverse economic outcomes. Russia prior to its dissolution in the later twentieth century maintained a rich and powerful political elite while much of the population struggled economically. The much lauded countries of Denmark, Norway, and Sweden practice forms of social democracy and produce various economic outcomes.

We must take into serious consideration the economic positions of individual incomes and wealth which depend upon a number of factors to include geographic locations, outcomes, and enjoyment. Various outcomes will be beneficial to all types of individuals as these outcomes can produces greater opportunities for individual interaction and exchange of items of value. These varying outcomes demonstrate the need of humility between individuals as well. Humility which signifies one individual can never possess the totality of knowledge, resources, and skills necessary for human flourishing. Individuals in a particular economic environment need one another.

Economic justice for individuals is achieved when individuals have the freedom to choose with whom they interact and make decisions which best align with their particular needs ultimately producing various expressions of enjoyment.

330 Million Visions

"The tragic vision is a vision of trade-offs, rather than solutions, and a vision of wisdom distilled from the experiences of the many, rather than the brilliance of a few."

Thomas Sowell

Archbishop Desmond Tutu offered a stellar example of the importance of recognizing our sacred dignity using the South African principle called ubuntu. What is ubuntu? It is the idea one human being has the capacity to demonstrate the sacredness of humanity to another. A human being has the freedom to actualize his or her potential and as a result other human beings will have the opportunity to benefit. Why? There is the belief of a universal thread which connects all of us. We have the capacity to create a beautiful tapestry for life. I understand this universal thread to be the imago Dei. Men and women created in the likeness of God, possessing the capacity and personality to produce for the good of the self and by extension the lives of others. Because of this interrelatedness and this indestructible powerful dignity which resides in all of us- transcending our economic and social barriers- we have the opportunity for synergistic affirmation. Imagine individuals having the maximum opportunity to become who he or she desires to become.

I have always defined vision as seeing the world as it is and then announcing how the world should be as a result of particular actions. We have visions for life. You may think of them as dreams or the materialization of your beliefs. We have visions for our life and we desire to achieve those visions regardless of our economic position in life. The question becomes, "Whose vision should prevail?"

Our shared human dignity brings about the realization every human being exists in a state of freedom. Our inherent dignity is woven with freedom because we are reflections of a Supreme Personality who is the freest of all beings. This reality offers us the confidence each individual regardless of economic situation has the capacity to determine for him or herself the course of life. We acknowledge as well there are men and women throughout history who have taken this freedom as a means to restrict the freedom of others, oppressing others in the dark hope of achieving some vision of reality. This is when visions clash in a society. There are numerous visions for life yet there are a few who have determined a singular vision should be the destiny of all. Our history is replete with examples of individuals who have determined their particular economic vision must triumph over all others. This triumph sadly has come at the cost of human life and freedom. When our shared human dignity is sacrificed for the sake of a particular economic vision determined by one individual or a select few, the vision itself has become a nightmare

The most difficult vision we have before us is a world in which people can determine for themselves a life with minimal obstacles and experiences of oppression. A difficult vision of individuals using freedom to align with the desires of the heart while not crushing the freedom and desires of others. We have a responsibility to maximize freedom for individuals and not pursue or support courses of action which ultimately create environments of injustice and oppression.

A difficult vision requires each of us learn what one individual desires in life and how to achieve those desires are more than likely not the same as his or her neighbor. The individual pursuit of desire which can not be quantified creates a level of discomfort. We are not comfortable with struggle, loss, a lack of influence, and worst of all, death. What reality demonstrates even in our current society, when individual men and women pursue a particular vision, the outcomes will be different. Are we willing to live in the discomfort individuals will choose different occupations leading to different financial outcomes? Are we willing to live in the discomfort individuals will learn differently and therefore, educational outcomes will be vary? We must be willing to live in the presence of difficult visions, individuals willing to choose for themselves a course of live which makes each happy. This does not suggest we should turn a blind eye to injustice, an individual not receiving what is due to him or herself. We should work together to maintain the precious and fragile environment which cultivates the growth of freedom among individuals leading to a prospering society. Thus, we should pursue ideas and policies which will rectify, minimize, and end activities obstructing the ability of individuals to actualize freedom and maximize in the lives of individuals opportunities which align with happiness.

Every day individuals, specifically individuals who are experiencing poverty, need greater exposure to the ideas of free participation and transactions within an economic environment. When individuals possess the opportunities to interact with whomever they choose and whenever they choose to achieve the vision for their individual lives, these individuals experience the greatest amount of exposure to cultivate cross-economic relationships, improve decision making, and find new opportunities to participate, if they are willing.

Special interest groups exist. Groups of individuals or organizations marshaling together to influence legislators to enact particular legislation at the expense of other nonparticipants. These special interest groups are called lobbyists, government bureaucrats, businesses, and people organizing around a particular goal. These groups participate in a system which encourages activities and legislation marginalizing and preventing others from sitting at the economic table. The invitation to discuss at the economic table does not arrive in the hands of individuals in poverty because special interest groups collaborate with the waiters-government-to consume the opportunities to produce and improve prosperity.

A difficult vision removes the power and privilege of special interest groups creating greater opportunities of participation among everyday individuals, especially those in poverty, so they can have greater freedom to accumulate wealth as each individual sees fit. Therefore, a difficult vision demands a level of personal responsibility on behalf of the poor to gather knowledge and demand participation, whereas, elected members of government reject opportunities to increase the power and privilege of a few.

We should not be ignorant. Individuals are created to exist in participation with other individuals. This is why we have groups of people in the form of families, worship communities, civic organizations, cities, towns, and states. We come together because we have the internal desire of communion with others. A beautiful society recognizes its dependence on the life and freedom of individuals. We have to participate in the hard work reminding one another our society depends on the existence of a diversity of lives who have the freedom to live, produce, and consume as they see fit while not harming the life and treasure of another.

The realization of freedom existing in all individuals can cultivate empathy in men and women across economic boundaries. Economic boundaries which can be crossed when any and all obstacles to such transitions are removed. As this happens, the society benefits. Imagine empathetic individuals using the means of freedom to engage in transactions which align with particular needs rather than coercion. The society can benefit from cross-cultural interactions which can diminish stereotypes. Interactions between various individuals from different ethnic backgrounds can create more opportunities for increased knowledge, the development of soft skills, and opportunities to add specific knowledge previously unknown to an individual. When we create obstacles and coercive activities to bring about one particular vision for life, we violate the human dignity of individuals. We become agents of injustice constructing obstacles to free participation through the implementation of policies and government action which isolate those in poverty from the larger societal and economic context. True justice will involve the protection of individual freedom to live and mature in accordance to his or her particular vision for life exciting the dignity and worth of human beings.

We are created in freedom. Men and women who are living reflections of a Supreme Personality who has happily chosen to have each of us participate in a vision which will reflect overwhelming happiness. Each of us have a particular vision of life which contributes to this larger vision of life. We have visions for our lives intended to be woven together creating a tapestry for the universe itself to stand and applaud. We are invited to participate and exercise our lives, personalities, and skills to discover our individual purposes in relationship to the purposes of others. We are created in freedom for the purpose of pursuing an enjoyment which if guarded and protected, will produce an affirmative proclamation of "Well done."

Notes

1. Ludwig von Mises, *Theory and History: An Interpretation of Social and Economic Evolution* (New Haven: Yale University Press, 1957), p.371.

2. Rufus Burrow, *Introduction to Personalism*, (Nashville:Chalice Press, 1999).

3. Rufus Burrow, *God and Human Dignity: The Personalism, Theology, and Ethics of Martin Luther King Jr.*, (Notre Dame: University of Notre Dame Press, 2006), p.74.

4. Jean Jacques Rousseau, *The Social Contract*, (London: Arcturus Publishing, 2018), p.47.

5. Tupac Shakur, *The Rose that Grew from Concrete*, (New York: Pocket Books, 1999), p.3.

6. Robert Nozick, *Anarchy, State, and Utopia*, (New York: Basic Books, 1974), p.297.

7. J. Cole, *KOD*, Dreamville Records. 2018. iTunes.

8. Richard Ebeling 1998. Introduction. Bastiat, F. *The Law*.

    (New York: Quality Books), xix.

9. Thomas Sowell, *Intellectuals and Society*, (New York: Basic

    Books, 2011), p.96.

About the Author

Phillip Demond Fletcher is the founder and director of CoHO, a non-profit organization in Conway, Arkansas as well as the founder of Humanity Matters, an organization engaged in teaching people what it means to be fully human from a Christian perspective. Phillip frequently speaks and writes on issues concerning the local church, leadership, and social justice. He is the author of *The Excellence of God: Essays in Theology and Doxology*. He has served as an appointee by Governor Asa Hutchinson to the 20th Judicial District Criminal Detention Facilities Review Committee. He serves as an appointee on the Conway Homeless Taskforce. He is a graduate of Arkansas State Chamber Leadership Class XII.

He holds an B.A. in Ethnic Studies from U.C. Riverside, M.A. in Theology from Liberty University, and a doctorate in Organizational Leadership from Regent University.

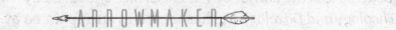

The Arrowmaker imprint is committed to affirming the dignity and worth of human beings in a manner that is loving, kind, thought provoking, and above all else, honoring to God. The mission for the Arrowmaker imprint is to publish works which are loving, kind, thought provoking, and God glorifying. The name of the imprint represents the last name of the Fletcher family who have committed themselves to sending out men and women to achieve their unique purposes in life through poverty alleviation, nonprofit development, and child birth advocacy.